Simple poems for little people

A short poetry book by M.D Head

This book is safe and suitable

for anyone of age.

Fly

I wish I was a bird,
flying high up in the sky,
It would be cool,
to see the world,
from a bird's eye.

Bath Time

When it's time to have my bath,
I smile big and wide,
for that's when I can sail my
boat,
that my rubber duck can ride.

My Kite

On windy days I fly my kite,
it's really quite a site,
I watch it dance,
as I hold the string,
with fingers gripping tight.

The Park

My friend and I went to the
park,
and played upon the swings,
there were lots of things,
on what to play,
some would work with springs.

Shapes

There are so many shapes,
be they circle or a square,
maybe a rectangle or triangle,
There are so many everywhere.

Brush Your Teeth

Brush your teeth every day,
make them clean and white,
then your enjoy your breakfast,
In the morning and at night.

Colours

I like the colour Red,
also the colour blue,
Brown and Black,
Green and purple,
They are good too.

Big and Small

Big things are great,
Small things are too,
like bubble gum that grows,
from a piece that's small.

Rocket

I flew my rocket,
to the stars,
I raced it past,
flying cars.

Hat

I love my hat,
it fits me well,
it makes me feel,
so great and swell

Cat and Dog

Cat and Dog,
went to the park,
Came home early,
avoiding the dark.

Superheros

Superheroes everywhere,
driving cars or in the air,
some can jump over your house,
Some can be small as a mouse.

Toy box

Our Toy box is great,
it's full of toys,
it's a treasure of wonders,
for girls and boys.

My Dog

My dog is so funny,
when it's time for his wash,
he soaks the bathroom,
with a splish,splash and splosh.

Holiday

We're going on holiday,
to explore places new,
ready for adventure,
you can come too.

The Carousel

I heard the music,
as the horses danced,
as children would ride,
the wooden animals that
pranced

The Zoo

Today I saw animals,
of every kind,
big and small,
sone mean and some kind.

Story time

Story time is great,
full of stories for all,
stories of fantasy,
myth so magical.

See Saw

Up and down,
down and up,
If you want to get down,
you need to go up.

Garden Helpers

When we go to sleep at night,
our garden gnomes,
work through the night.

Fruit and Veg

I really like fruit,
vegetables too,
they're all kinds of colours,
and so good for you.

Christmas Morning

On Christmas morning,
we looked at the tree,
full of tinsel and lights,
and gifts for you and me.

My Bicycle

Down with one pedal,
then up with another,
when I'm riding my bike,
I'm faster than my brother.

Houses

Some houses are short,
though some are tall,
some are really big,
some are really small.

Spinning top

Faster and faster,
it spins around,
when it will stop,
it will make a sound.

Clouds

I made faces,
in the clouds today,
clouds of white,
clouds of grey.

Shoe laces

I learnt to tie my laces today,
at first it was quite hard,
the more I practised every day,
the more it became less hard.

"I hope you enjoyed reading this books as much as i enjoyed writing it" - m.d head

M.D Head is an indie writer who spends
his spare time writing short books for all
ages. He started his journey when he
published his first novel "Notre Dame" and
then managed to compile his old poetry
since then he has blossomed into a writer
for all ages.

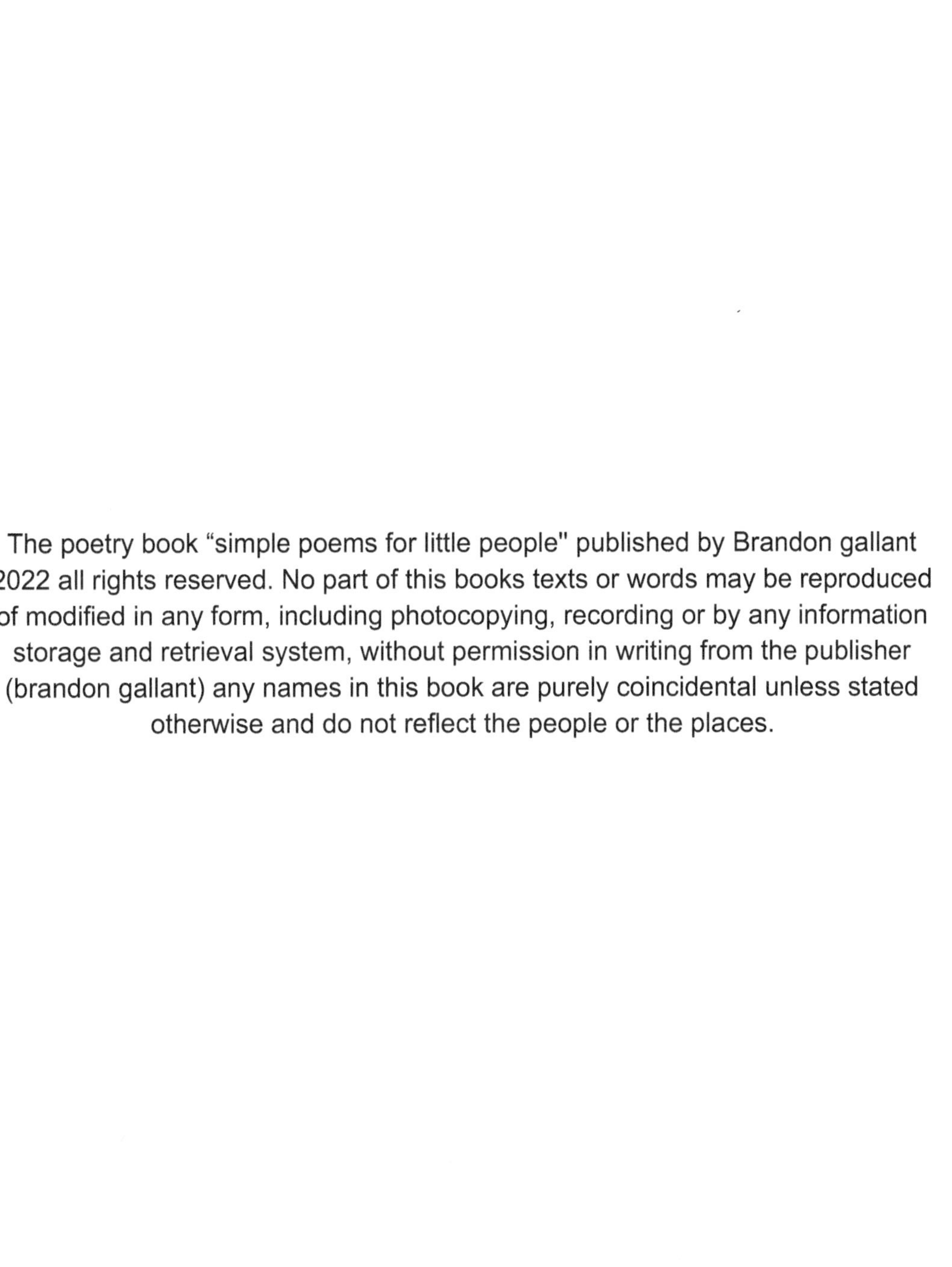